Forever Friends

A Record Book of Our Friendship

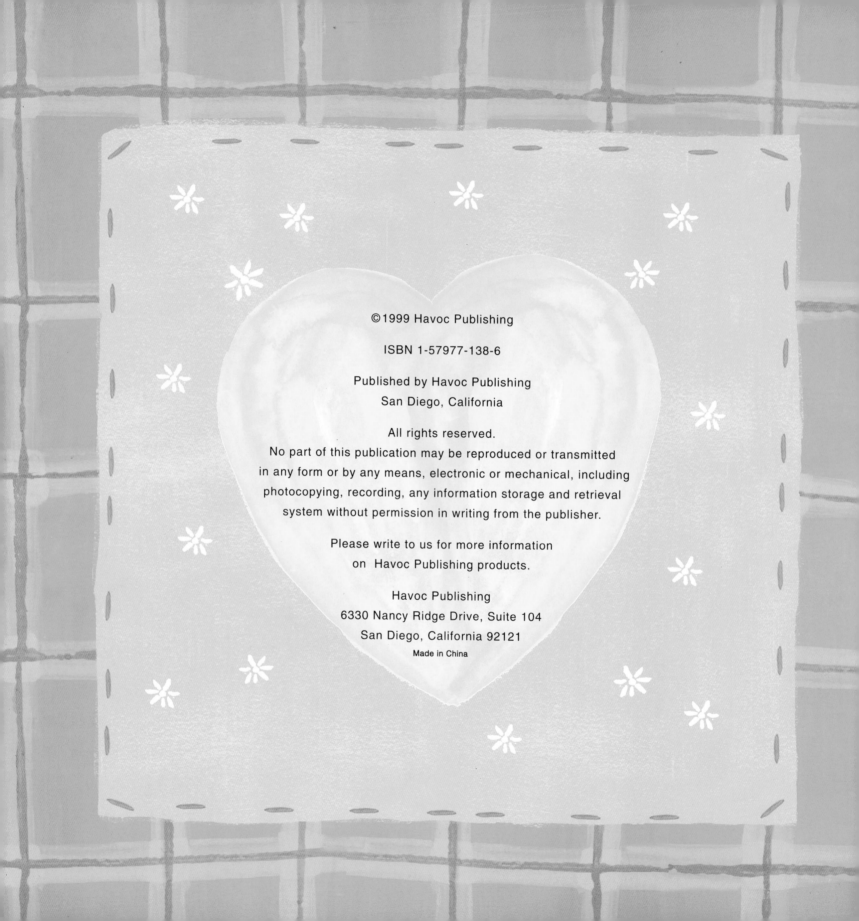

a record book for

....

and

....

Contents

Your birth date ....

Where you grew up ....

....

What you do in life ....

....

Your education ....

....

Your family ....

....

....

....

....

How We Met

The day we met _____

_____

What was happening in the news _____

_____

Where we met _____

_____

_____

How we were introduced to each other _____

_____

_____

_____

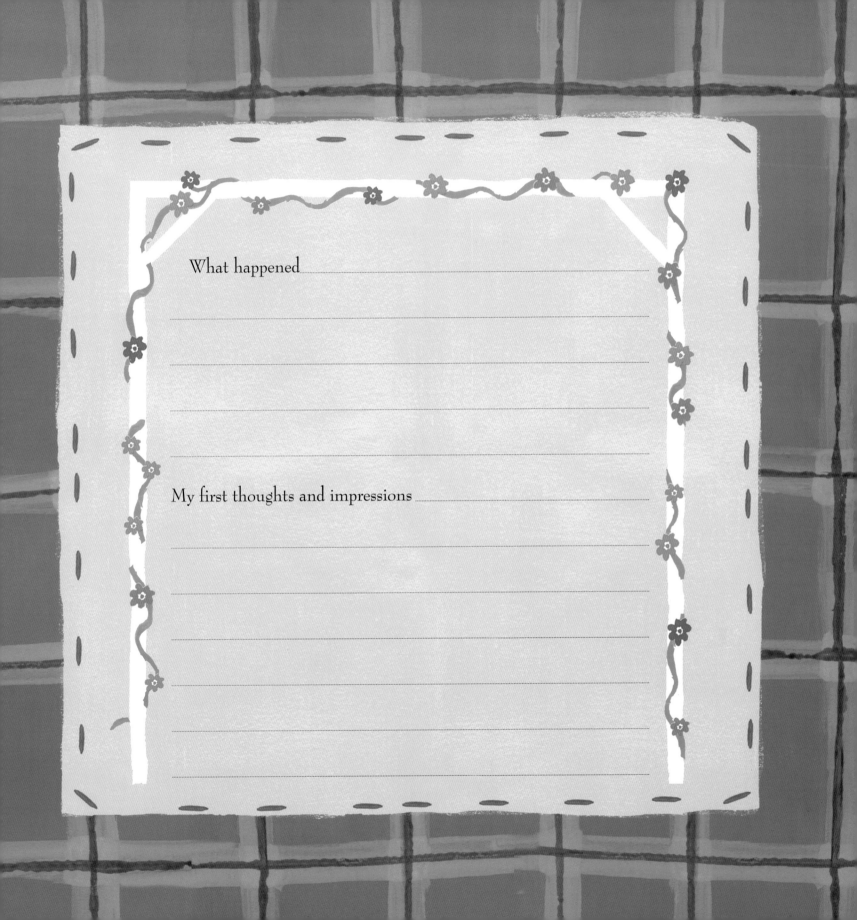

What happened ....

....

....

....

....

My first thoughts and impressions ....

....

....

....

....

....

Our Blossoming Friendship

What made us compatible _____

_____

_____

_____

What we liked most about eachother _____

_____

_____

When we knew we would be friends _____

_____

_____

Photograph

Photograph

We Are Alike...

How we are alike _____

_____

_____

_____

Things we like to do together _____

_____

_____

_____

_____

_____

How we are different ....

_____

_____

_____

_____

My type of man ....

Things we should do separately ....

_____

_____

Your type of man ....

_____

_____

Yet Totally Different!

What We Love

Films ....

Celebrities ....

Authors ....

Artists ....

Performers ....

Desserts ....

Drinks ....

Restaurants ....

....

The way people . . . _____

_____

When parents . . . _____

_____

When co-workers . . . _____

_____

When neighbors . . . _____

_____

When clothes . . . _____

_____

When people wear . . . _____

_____

What Bugs Us

Girls' Night Out

What we like to do _____

_____

_____

Favorite restaurants _____

_____

_____

_____

Favorite hang-outs _____

_____

_____

Friends we like to go out with _____

_____

_____

_____

_____

Best event we ever attended _____

_____

_____

Why it was the best ....

....

Worst event we ever attended, and why ....

....

....

Best time we've had getting ready to go out ....

....

....

Who takes the longest to get ready, and why ....

....

Starlight Lane

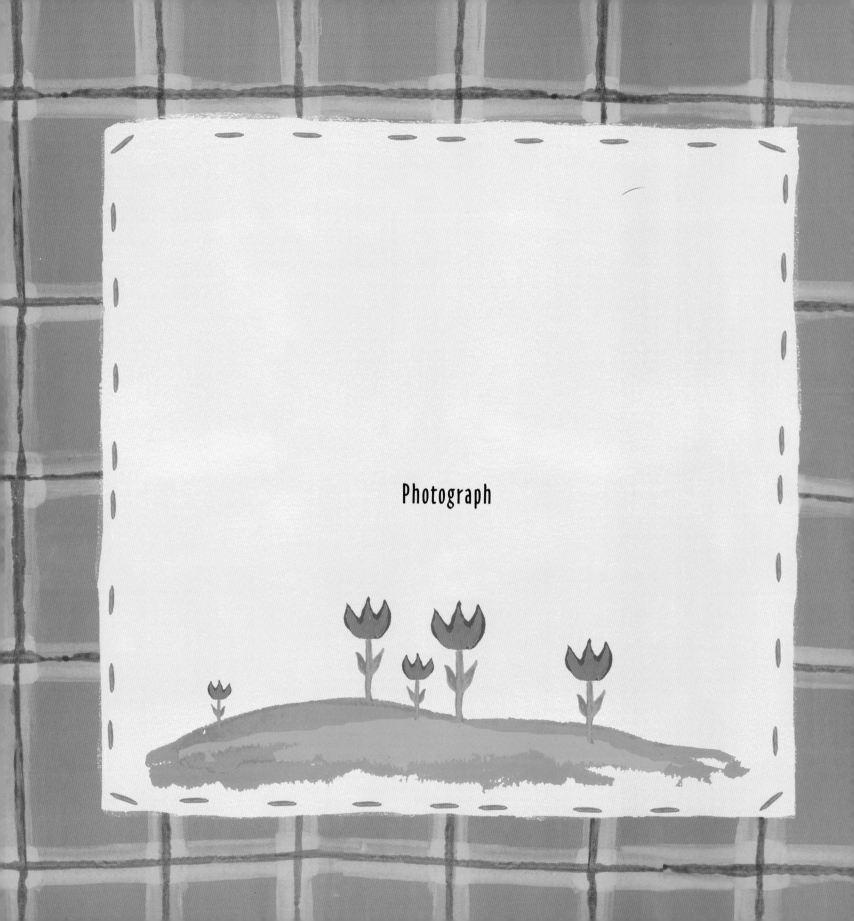

Photograph

Photograph

Moments

Some of our craziest moments _____
_____
_____
_____
_____
_____
_____
_____
_____
_____
_____
_____

Advise

Hot tips I got from you _____

_____

_____

_____

_____

_____

_____

_____

_____

_____

_____

Dishin' It Out

Tips that went sour

Can You Believe That Happened?

Unbelievable adventures _____

_____

_____

_____

_____

_____

_____

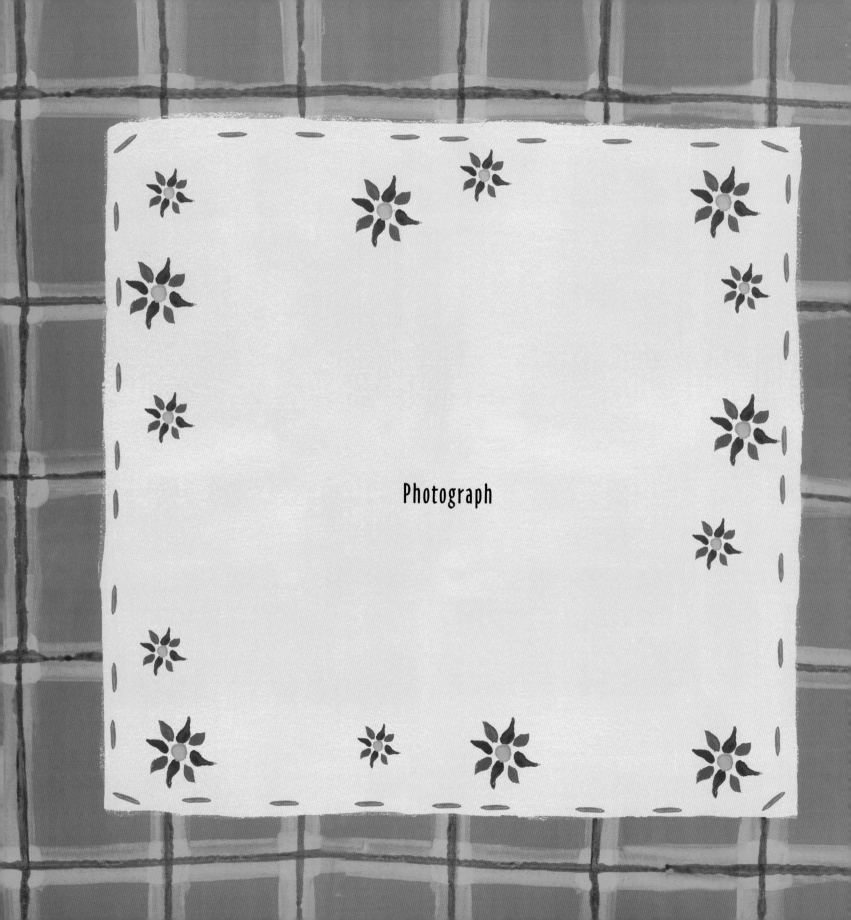

Photograph

Photograph

Traveling...

Our most memorable trip _____

Our funniest travel story _____

and Hanging Out

Things we like to do together _____

_____

_____

_____

Places we like to go together _____

_____

_____

_____

Photo

Favorite lazy afternoon activities _____

_____

_____

Fun Times Together

Remember when _____

_____

_____

_____

_____

_____

_____

_____

Remember when _____

_____

_____

_____

_____

_____

_____

_____

_____

Above & Beyond the Call

You stood by me when _____

_____

_____

_____

I stood by you when _____

_____

_____

_____

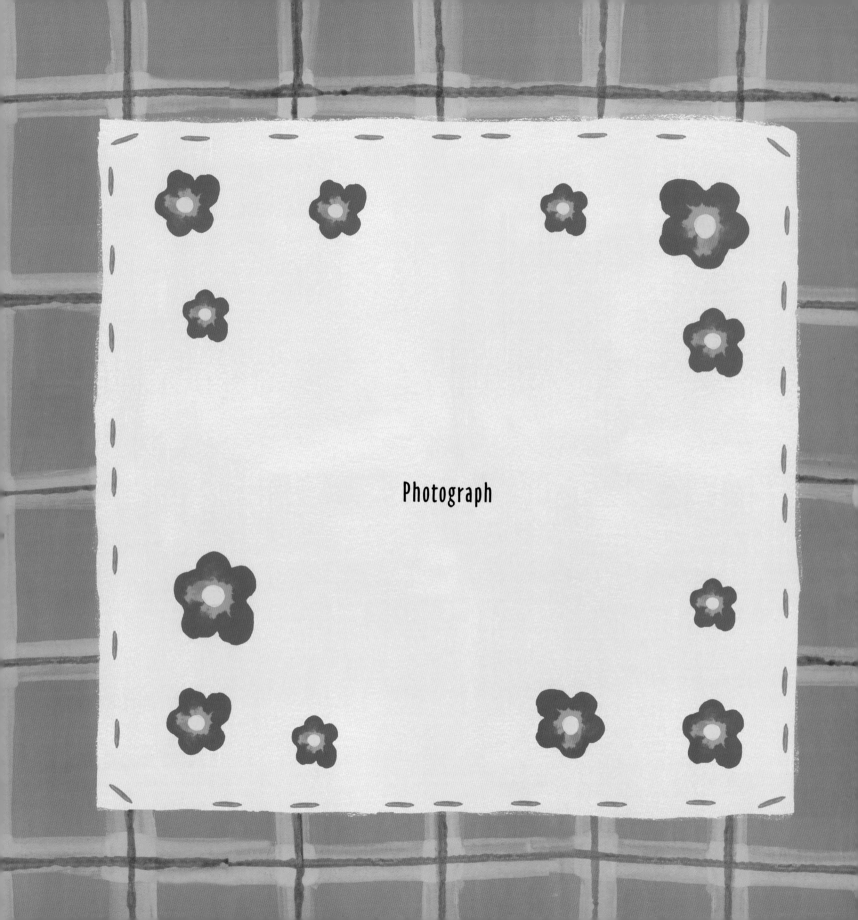

Photograph

Photograph

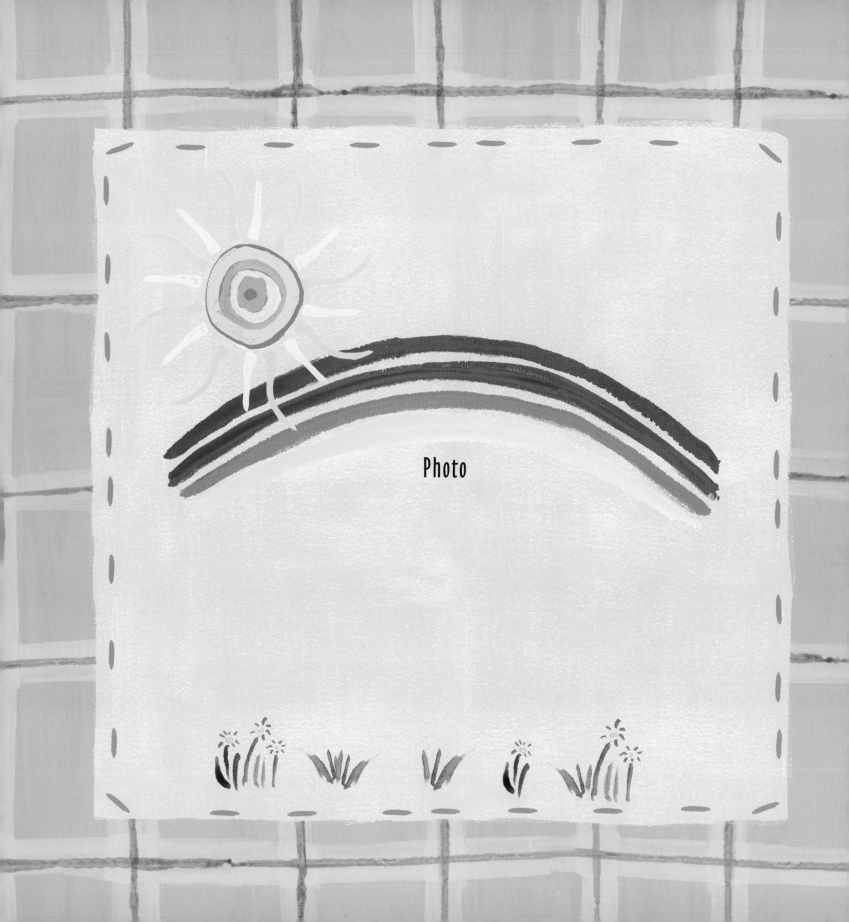

Photo

My Favorite Story About You

Remember the Time...

When we called _____

_____

When we drove _____

_____

When we dated _____

_____

When we danced _____

_____

When we _____

_____

Photo

We Had a Blast!

We had the best time when _____

_____

_____

_____

_____

_____

_____

_____

_____

Photograph

Photograph

Learning From Each Other

Over the years, I taught you _____

_____

_____

_____

_____

_____

_____

_____

_____

_____

_____

Over the years, you taught me _____

_____

_____

_____

_____

_____

_____

_____

_____

_____

Dates to Remember

Birthdays _____   Anniversaries _____

_____   _____

_____   _____

Graduations _____   Weddings _____

_____   _____

_____   _____

Births _____   Other _____

_____   _____

_____   _____

Can I Borrow Your...

Remember the time I wore your _____

_____

_____

_____

I can't believe I ruined your _____

_____

_____

_____

I always wanted to borrow your _____

_____

_____

_____

I still owe you _____

_____

_____

_____

Photograph

Photograph

Shop 'Til We Drop!

Favorite malls _____

_____

Best buys _____

_____

Longest days spent shopping _____

_____

I always seem to be looking for _____

_____

You always seem to be looking for _____

_____

_____

Favorite shopping story

Photo

Stayin' Healthy

Favorite outdoor workout places _____

_____

Favorite indoor workout places _____

_____

Favorite exercises _____

_____

Favorite way to pamper ourselves _____

_____

Hangin' with All the Girls

Special places we go _____

_____

_____

_____

_____

_____

_____

_____

_____

_____

How we all met _____

_____

_____

Memorable group events _____

_____

_____

_____

_____

Photo

Photograph

Photograph

Photo

Tomorrow's Dreams

Available Record Books from Havoc

Baby	Mom
Coach	Mothers & Daughters
College Life	My Pregnancy
Couples	Our Honeymoon
Dad	Retirement
Family	School Days
Forever Friends	Single Life
Girlfriends	Sisters
Golf	Teacher
Grandmother	Traveling Adventures
Grandparents	Tying the Knot

Please write to us with your ideas for
additional Havoc Publishing products

Havoc Publishing
6330 Nancy Ridge Drive, Suite 104
San Diego, CA 92121